Great
Rivers
of the World

THE MISSISSIPPI

Kieran Walsh

WORLD ALMANAC® LIBRARY

Please visit our web site at: www.worldalmanaclibrary.com
For a free color catalog describing World Almanac® Library's list of high-quality books and multimedia programs, call 1-800-848-2928 (USA) or 1-800-387-3178 (Canada). World Almanac® Library's fax: (414) 332-3567.

Library of Congress Cataloging-in-Publication Data

Walsh, Kieran.
    The Mississippi / Kieran J. Walsh.
       p. cm. — (Great rivers of the world)
    Includes bibliographical references and index.
    Contents: The course of the river — The Mississippi in history — Cities and settlements — Economic activity — Animals and plants — Environmental issues — Leisure and recreation — The future.
    ISBN 0-8368-5444-6 (lib. bdg.)
    ISBN 0-8368-5451-9 (softcover)
    1. Mississippi River—Juvenile literature. 2. Mississippi River Valley—Juvenile literature.
[1. Mississippi River. 2. Mississippi River Valley.] I. Title. II. Series.
    F351.W28   2003
    977—dc21
                                2002034315

First published in 2003 by
World Almanac® Library
330 West Olive Street, Suite 100
Milwaukee, WI 53212 USA

Developed by Monkey Puzzle Media
Editor: Jane Bingham
Designer: Mark Whitchurch
Picture researcher: Sally Neal
World Almanac® Library editor: Jim Mezzanotte
World Almanac® Library art direction: Tammy Gruenewald

Picture acknowledgements
AKG London, 14, 15; Alamy, 7 (Third Eye Images), 23 (M. Friang), 26–27 (B. Atkinson); John Cole, 19; Corbis, front cover (Philip Gould), 8 (David Muench), 9 (O. Franken), 10 (Dave G. Houser), 20 (Bill Ross), 21 (David Muench), 27 top (David Hamilton Smith), 35 (Philip Gould), 45 (Annie Griffiths Belt); Digital Vision, 1, 25; Eye Ubiquitous, 4–5 (L. Fordyce), 11 (L. Fordyce), 17 (L. Fordyce), 36 (L. Fordyce); James Davis Travel Photography, 42; Mary Evans Picture Library, 12, 13; Robert Harding Picture Library, 30 (Robert Francis), 31 (Robert McLeod), 32 (Photri); Still Pictures, 29 (Alex Maclean), 33 (John Cancalosi), 34 (William Campbell), 37 (Peter Arnold); Topham Picturepoint, 16 (Image Works), 28 (Image Works), 38–39 (Image Works), 40 (Image Works); Travel Ink, 22 (Ronald Badkin). Map artwork by Peter Bull.

Printed in the United States of America

1 2 3 4 5 6 7 8 9 07 06 05 04 03

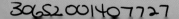

CONTENTS

CONTENTS

	Introduction	4
1	The Course of the River	6
2	The Mississippi in History	12
3	Cities and Settlements	18
4	Economic Activity	24
5	Animals and Plants	30
6	Environmental Issues	34
7	Leisure and Recreation	40
8	The Future	44
	Glossary	46
	Time Line	47
	Further Information	47
	Index	48

INTRODUCTION
INTRODUCTION

The Mighty Mississippi

The Mississippi River is the most important waterway in North America. By the time the first European settlers arrived on the continent, Native Americans had already been living on the banks of the river and traveling its course for centuries.

The river flows north to south, roughly down the middle of the North American continent. Its entire course is in the United States, and it serves as an unofficial dividing line between the eastern and western halves of the country. Places in the United States are often referred to as being east or west of the Mississippi River.

Several rivers, called **tributaries**, feed into the Mississippi, and because these tributaries lead both east and west, the river serves as an ideal shipping route for much of the North American heartland. Several tributaries are almost as long, or longer, than the Mississippi, which is 2,348 miles (3,778 kilometers) long. The Missouri River, for example, which is the Mississippi's longest tributary, has a length of 2,566 miles (4,129 km). The combined Missouri-Mississippi river system is the third longest in the world, after the Nile and the Amazon river systems.

The Heart of the U.S.A.

The Mississippi starts as a trickle in the state of Minnesota, but it grows to be over a mile wide at some points before it empties into the Gulf of Mexico. On its journey, the Mississippi and the rivers flowing into it drain water from thirty-one states. In doing so, the Mississippi carries an incredible amount of **sediment** to the sea.

Over 12 million people live in communities along the Mississippi River, and another 4 million people who do not live near the river still rely upon the Mississippi for their water supply. In one way or another, the lives of a huge number of people in the United States are connected to the Mississippi River. For many, it is not just a river, but a living thing.

The Mississippi winds past cities, small towns, open countryside, and woodland before it finally reaches the sea.

> **"** *The Mississippi River remains what it always was — a kind of huge rope, no matter with what knots and frayings, tying the United States together. It is the Nile of the Western Hemisphere.* **"**
>
> Historian John Gunther,
> *Inside USA* (1947)

MISSISSIPPI FACTS

- Length: 2,348 miles (3,778 km)
- Drainage basin: 1.2 million square miles (3.1 million square kilometers)
- Main cities: Minneapolis (Minnesota), St. Paul (Minnesota), St. Louis (Missouri), Memphis (Tennessee), Baton Rouge (Louisiana), New Orleans (Louisiana)
- Major tributaries: Missouri, 2,566 miles (4,130 km); Arkansas, 1,450 miles (2,333 km); Ohio, 982 miles (1,580 km)

Chapter 1

THE COURSE OF THE RIVER

How the Mississippi Was Formed

The Mississippi River as we know it today was formed during the last ice age, which began roughly 12,000 years ago. At this time, massive, slowly moving sheets of ice, called glaciers, covered most of North America. The glaciers had begun at the North Pole and traveled south, plowing loads of sediment into North America like huge shovels.

One patch of North America, known as the Driftless Region, was not covered by glaciers. This territory included most of present-day Minnesota, Wisconsin, Iowa, and Illinois. Scientists believe huge areas of depressed land north of the Driftless Region protected it from glaciers. At the end of the last ice age, when the glaciers melted, the areas of land became Lake Superior, Lake Michigan, and Green Bay.

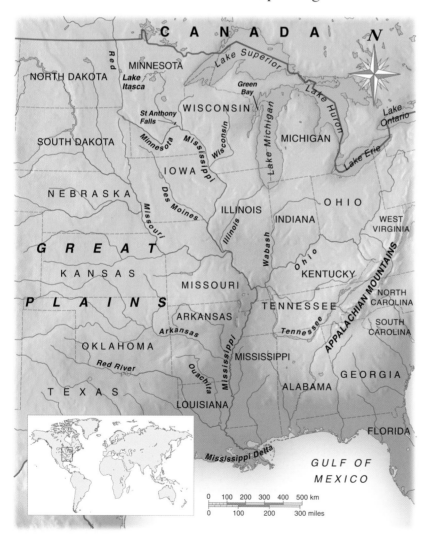

This map shows the course of the Mississippi and its main tributaries.

6

The River Starts to Flow

When glaciers melted, the Driftless Region flooded with water. The glaciers melted slowly, so this water was filled with chunks of hard, jagged ice, as well as dirt and soil the glaciers had carried down from the North Pole. Two major mountain ranges — the Rockies in the west and the Appalachians in the east — forced this water to travel south. As the water flowed, the ice remaining in it carved out the path of the Mississippi River.

THE LAST ICE AGE

The term ice age refers to a period of time in Earth's history when much of it was covered by ice. Earth has experienced several ice ages, but the last ice age, also known as the Pleistocene era, began around 130,000 years ago and ended roughly 10,000 years ago. During this period, most of the North American continent was covered by a series of glaciers.

New Land

Over time, the Mississippi filled with sediment. Some sediment ended up on the bottom of the river, and some was distributed on the riverbanks, where it helped to create rich soil ideal for farming. The river carried so much sediment, in fact, that the sediment formed a new portion of land. As the sediment emptied into the Gulf of Mexico, it created an area of flat land — the Mississippi River **delta**.

Waves crash on the shore of Lake Superior. The lake was originally an area of land on the northern edge of the Driftless Region, where the Mississippi River was formed during the last ice age.

Upper and Lower

The Mississippi is usually divided into two parts — an upper (northern) half and a lower (southern) half. The Upper Mississippi refers to the stretch of river from Lake Itasca in Minnesota, which is the river's **source**, to Thebes, Illinois. This stretch of the river incorporates Minnesota, Wisconsin, Iowa, Illinois, and Missouri. The Lower Mississippi refers to the stretch of river from Thebes to the river's **mouth** on the Gulf of Mexico, and it incorporates Kentucky, Tennessee, Arkansas, Mississippi, and Louisiana.

The upper stretch of the Mississippi River begins at Lake Itasca in Minnesota.

The climates of the Upper and Lower Mississippi are very different. The **basin** of the Upper Mississippi is generally cool, while the Lower Mississippi basin is warmer. The temperatures for the Mississippi River delta are particularly warm, ranging from 60° to 80° Fahrenheit (16° to 27° Celsius).

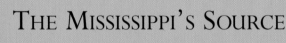

THE MISSISSIPPI'S SOURCE

As the Mississippi River grew in importance to European settlers, a number of expeditions were launched to find its source. Not until 1832, however, did an explorer named Henry Rowe Schoolcraft discover that the Mississippi River starts at a lake in Minnesota. Schoolcraft named the lake Itasca by combining parts of two Latin words — *veritas,* which means "true," and *caput,* which means "head."

Changing Landscapes

As the waters of the Mississippi flow southward, they pass through many different landscapes. From Lake Itasca to St. Anthony Falls near Minneapolis, the Mississippi flows through part of the Great Plains, a region of the Midwest with few hills. The Mississippi River **meanders** lazily through the region's flat land, and its waters are generally calm.

At the St. Anthony Falls, the waters of the Mississippi come violently to life, racing between sharp cliffs and crags in Iowa, Wisconsin, and Illinois. In Tennessee the river becomes calm, and its waters flow leisurely through cotton fields. At Vicksburg, in the state of Mississippi, the river is flanked once again by steep cliffs.

The last stage before the Mississippi finishes its course to the sea is the Mississippi delta. The delta looks different than any other region through which the river passes — it is an area of hot, marshy swamps called bayous. Beyond the delta, the waters of the Mississippi River reach the Gulf of Mexico and eventually join the Atlantic Ocean.

The Mississippi delta, near the point where the river reaches the sea at the Gulf of Mexico, has many bayous. The delta's climate is warm and humid all year.

The River's Tributaries

On a map, the Mississippi River and its tributaries resemble a tree with many branches spreading in different directions. The Mississippi has over forty tributaries, many of which are major rivers in their own right. Six main tributaries — the Arkansas, Illinois, Minnesota, Missouri, Ohio, and Wisconsin Rivers — form the Mississippi River system.

The Missouri River

The Missouri River, which is the Mississippi's longest tributary and is actually longer than the Mississippi itself, has it source in Yellowstone National Park in Wyoming. In Montana, the river joins with the waters of Fort Peck Lake, and at St. Louis, Missouri, it connects with the Mississippi. The Missouri River has several tributaries of its own, and each spring they force tons of sediment into the river. The Missouri's sediment has earned it the nickname "Big Muddy." Sediment from the Missouri River probably helped create the Mississippi River delta.

Fireboats are used to put out fires on or near the Mississippi and Missouri Rivers. This fireboat is jetting the muddy waters of the Missouri high into the air.

A Growing River

From Lake Itasca to St. Paul, Minnesota, the Mississippi River is a relatively small stream, but beyond its meeting point with the Missouri River it begins to grow. The Ohio River, which begins in Pittsburgh, Pennsylvania, and meets the Mississippi at Cairo, Illinois, adds even more water to the river. After meeting the Ohio River, the Mississippi swells, measuring up to 1.5 miles (2.4 km) from bank to bank.

The Arkansas River is the last major tributary on the Mississippi's course to the sea. The river begins in the Rocky Mountains of Colorado and meets the Mississippi in Greenville, Mississippi. With a length of 1,450 miles (2,333 km), the Arkansas River is nearly as long as the Mississippi and Missouri Rivers.

With the water it receives from its tributaries, the Mississippi River grows from a stream into a large, powerful river. In addition to supplying the Mississippi with water, the tributaries connect the river to many regions of the United States.

At Cairo, Illinois, the Ohio River joins the Mississippi River.

Chapter 2

THE MISSISSIPPI IN HISTORY

THE MISSISSIPPI IN HISTORY

Native Americans

Experts believe people were living along the Mississippi River about 11,500 years ago. These people relied on the river for their food and water. They hunted the bison that lived on the riverbanks, and they traveled along the Mississippi in their canoes.

The high point of early civilization along the Mississippi was the Mississippian culture, which flourished roughly 1,000 years ago. At one time, the region where Cahokia, Illinois, stands today was the center of this culture. The region had an estimated population of 10,000 to 20,000 Native Americans.

The exact fate of the region's inhabitants is not clear. A gradual decline in their numbers began sometime after 1200, and by the 1400s, the area had been abandoned. Most scholars believe floods and diseases, such as smallpox, caused widespread death. The inhabitants did leave behind earth mounds, which still exist today. These mounds are similar to ancient Egyptian pyramids in that they probably served as spiritual temples and burial places. The mounds vary in size, but the largest one, Monks Mound, measures 105 feet (32 meters) by 49 feet (15 m).

The Mississippi has always been a source of food for those who live near it. This painting depicts an imagined scene from a time before Europeans arrived in North America. In it, Native Americans are fishing on the river.

European Explorers

The first European to find the Mississippi was the Spanish explorer Hernando de Soto, who came to North America in 1539 searching for a city called El Dorado. De Soto never found El Dorado because it only existed in legend. He did, however, find the Mississippi, near present-day Memphis, Tennessee. De Soto died in 1542, before he could return to Europe. His men buried him in the waters of the Mississippi.

In 1673, the French explorers Louis Jolliet and Jacques Marquette set out to explore the Mississippi. The purpose of their expedition was to see if the Mississippi led west to the Gulf of California. Jolliet and Marquette traveled on the Mississippi to the mouth of the Arkansas River. In present-day Arkansas, they met Native Americans who told them the Mississippi flowed south.

Another Frenchman, René-Robert Cavalier, Sieur de La Salle, led the first successful mission down the Mississippi to the Gulf of Mexico. La Salle claimed the entire Mississippi River basin for France in 1682. He named the area "Louisiana" in honor of King Louis XIV of France.

BIG RIVER

The Ojibwe (Chippewa) Indians were one of the Native American peoples to live along the Mississippi River. The name Mississippi comes from an Ojibwe name for the river, *Meschasipi*, which means "Big River."

Hernando de Soto, a Spanish soldier and explorer, led the first European expedition to reach the Mississippi River.

The Louisiana Purchase

The Mississippi River basin changed hands a few times before it officially became part of the United States. La Salle had claimed the Mississippi basin for France, but it was taken over by the Spanish in 1769. Then, in 1800, it became French territory again.

In 1783, the Treaty of Paris formally freed the American colonists from British rule. The treaty declared the Mississippi River to be the western border of the United States. This border remained until 1803, when France sold a massive area of land to the United States. This territory began at the Mississippi River and stretched as far west as the Rocky Mountains. The sale of this region, known as the Louisiana Purchase, had a huge impact on the United States. With the addition of this territory, the size of the new nation practically doubled.

Steamboats and Traders

In 1811, the *New Orleans* became the first steamboat to sail on the Mississippi. Travel by steamboat was cheaper and easier than overland travel, which, for routes to and from the East Coast, usually involved a difficult cross over the Appalachian Mountains, so people began shipping goods via the Mississippi River and the Gulf of Mexico.

This painting shows a group of steamboats working their way up the river in 1866. In the lower left corner of the painting, a group of people at a landing stage have lit a fire to indicate they want to be picked up by a boat.

Steamboat production multiplied. As the new shipping industry grew, towns and **trading posts** sprang up along the Mississippi River. By the mid-1800s, the city of New Orleans, which is located in the Mississippi delta at the southern tip of Louisiana, was one of the busiest ports in the United States.

Civil War

Trade and shipping along the Mississippi River were interrupted by the Civil War, which lasted from 1861 to 1865. During the war, river traffic from the north virtually ceased. Since the Mississippi was such an important river, both the Union and the Confederacy tried to control it. In 1863, U.S. general Ulysses S. Grant claimed the Mississippi for the Union. Two years later, the Civil War ended.

> " The steamboats were finer than anything on shore. When a citizen stepped on board a big, fine steamboat, he entered a new and marvelous world. "
>
> Mark Twain, *Life on the Mississippi* (1883)

The Railroads Arrive

In the years after the Civil War, the Mississippi enjoyed a brief return to boom times, but the river soon faced new competition from railroads. Boats on the Mississippi could only travel north and south, but trains could travel east and west. As more people moved west, railroads replaced steamboats as the most important means of transportation.

This photo, taken in 1866, shows one of the new railroad lines that had begun to spring up across the United States. The railroads were able to reach a wider area than the river, and businesses soon began to use them to transport their goods.

Twentieth-Century Revival

River trade on the Mississippi River experienced a revival in the twentieth century. This revival was due to several factors, one being wartime production. During both World War I (1914–1918) and World War II (1939–1945), the manufacture of planes, guns, and other military supplies increased dramatically. During wartime, the Mississippi River was an important shipping route, and factories along it were vital producers of chemicals, diamonds, and lumber.

Another factor in the revival of trade on the river was the replacement of steamboats with barges and towboats, which were much more efficient. The shipping industry continued to grow, even during the Great Depression of the 1930s, when most of the United States was experiencing extreme poverty. It has been estimated that traffic on the Mississippi in 1931 was twice as heavy as at any time in the 1800s.

Barges are still widely used on the Mississippi to carry goods up and down the river. In this photograph, towboats create "rafts" of barges that are all headed to the same destination.

❝ *As the word Abraham means 'the father of a great multitude of men,' so the word Mississippi means 'the father of a great multitude of waters.' His tribes stream in from east and west, exceedingly fruitful the lands they enrich. In this granary of a continent, this basin of the Mississippi, will not the nations be greatly multiplied and blest?* ❞
Herman Melville, *The Confidence-Man: His Masquerade* (1857)

The Mississippi River Commission

Throughout the twentieth century, the Mississippi was improved and maintained by the Mississippi River Commission (MRC). Created in 1879 by an act of Congress, the commission has been responsible for some extraordinary work on the river. The commission has built dams and **locks**, widened channels, and constructed **levees** to control floods.

No amount of work, however, can tame nature. In both 1927 and 1993, catastrophic floods took place on the Mississippi River. Several hundred people were killed during these floods.

The Great River Road Parkway

In 1938, the U.S. government introduced a plan called the Great River Road Parkway. This plan was originally intended as a major road construction project to keep people employed during the Great Depression, but the project was eventually completed by simply improving existing roads and linking them together. The Great River Road Parkway runs from Canada to the Gulf of Mexico. It incorporates two highways — Route 61 in Minnesota and Route 35 in Wisconsin — and many smaller roads along or near both banks of the Mississippi River. Signs displaying a green and white pilot's wheel indicate roads that are part of the Great River Road Parkway.

The Mississippi River Commission (MRC) builds and maintains dams, such as this one in Missouri. Responsible for managing the Mississippi River, the MRC attempts to prevent disastrous floods and keeps the river clear for traffic.

The parkway has a length of almost 3,000 miles (4,828 km). Along the parkway, there are 87 federal parks, 1,100 sites that are listed in the National Registry of Historic Places (areas of historical importance that are protected by the National Park Service), and more than 150 visitor centers and museums. The Great River Road is a fitting tribute to the United States' greatest river.

Chapter 3

CITIES AND SETTLEMENTS

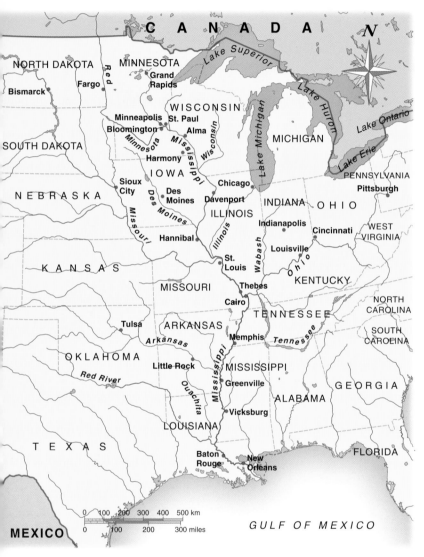

This map shows the main cities and towns along the Mississippi River.

Small Towns

The Mississippi River is linked to a number of large, famous cities. Cities, though, are only part of the picture. Many small towns on the Mississippi have equally rich histories.

While the cities of the Mississippi pave the way to the future, small towns are in many ways a reminder of the river's past. For the people who live in these communities, daily life is slower, calmer, and less crowded than in the big cities. The town of Alma, Wisconsin, for example, has a population of under a thousand people. Towns such as Alma help make up "small town America."

Several large cities on the Mississippi, such as St. Louis and New Orleans, thrive on **service industries**. Many of the people who live in the smaller communities along the river travel to the big cities to work in such service industry businesses as hotels, restaurants, and stores. In the city of Bloomington, Minnesota, hospitality is the number one service industry. The city's thirty-five restaurants and hotels, as well as the enormous Mall of America, employ more than 20,000 people from surrounding areas.

Links to the Past

A strong reminder of the past can be found in places such as Harmony, Minnesota, and Stockholm, Wisconsin, where large communities of Amish people live. The Amish are a religious group who do not believe in using radios, television sets, or other modern devices that depend on electricity. Most of the Amish make their living as farmers. All their farming is done either by hand or with horse-drawn equipment. For transportation, the Amish use horses and buggies — travel by car is not allowed. Kerosene lamps provide the lighting in Amish homes.

Mark Twain

The American writer Mark Twain has very strong links with the Mississippi River. Twain was born November 30, 1835, in Florida, Missouri. When he was four years old, his family moved to Hannibal, Missouri, a town on the banks of the Mississippi. Twain grew up dreaming of becoming a steamboat pilot, and he eventually received a license in 1859 and spent two years piloting cargo boats. In 1861, however, the Civil War broke out. Until the war ended, in 1865, very little commercial shipping occurred on the Mississippi, so Twain had to find other work as a newspaper reporter.

Mules tow an Amish farmer's machinery across a field. Amish people try not to use modern technology in their way of life. The Amish lifestyle provides a glimpse of what life was probably like for people on the Mississippi River 200 years ago.

Twain's real name was Samuel Langhorne Clemens. In his early days as a writer, he began using the name "Mark Twain," which was actually a phrase used by Mississippi boat pilots that means "two fathoms (12 feet, or 3.7 m) deep." Many of Twain's best-loved works center on the Mississippi, including *The Adventures of Tom Sawyer*, *Life on the Mississippi*, and *The Adventures of Huckleberry Finn*. Twain died in 1910.

Minneapolis and St. Paul

The Upper Mississippi basin is home to many famous cities. The state of Minnesota, for example, has two large riverfront cities — Minneapolis and St. Paul. Known collectively as the "Twin Cities," Minneapolis and St. Paul lie on opposite sides of the Mississippi. Minneapolis lies to the west of the river, while St. Paul lies to the east.

Like the Mississippi, the city of Minneapolis was given its name by Native Americans. *Minne* means "water." It is an appropriate name, because Minneapolis developed largely around St. Anthony Falls. The only large waterfall along the Mississippi, St. Anthony Falls has always been appreciated for its awesome beauty. At the end of the nineteenth century, however, people began using the falls to create electricity from water power. With power provided by St. Anthony Falls, Minneapolis became a leading city in both flour and lumber milling.

St. Paul is the capital of Minnesota. The city developed where it did because for many years it was the end point of steamboat travel up the Mississippi. It is the center of Minnesota's business and government and has an attractive downtown riverfront that includes parks, walkways, and restaurants.

BIRTH OF THE ICE CREAM CONE

At the 1904 World's Fair in St. Louis, Missouri, a man named Charles E. Minches had a booth where he sold ice cream in dishes. The day of July 23, 1904, was a hot one, and people at the fair were buying so much ice cream from Minches that he ran out of dishes. He went to a nearby stand, where his friend, Ernest Hamwi, was selling a Middle Eastern treat called zalabia. Zalabia is like a flat, crispy waffle. Minches began wrapping up his ice cream in zalabia, thus accidentally inventing what we now call the ice cream cone.

The Mississippi flows past downtown Minneapolis. This photo was taken from the city of St. Paul, which lies on the opposite bank of the river.

The Gateway Arch in St. Louis welcomes visitors to the city. It was designed by the Finnish architect Eero Saarinen. Completed in 1966, the arch is 630 feet (192 m) high and 630 feet (192 m) wide and can be seen from over 30 miles (48 km) away.

St. Louis

Further down the river, in the state of Missouri, lies the city of St. Louis. The city has been the site of many famous events in U.S. history. In 1846, a slave named Dred Scott filed a suit for his freedom at the St. Louis Circuit Court. When, in 1857, the Supreme Court ruled that Scott must remain a slave, the decision added to the rising tension between the antislavery northern states and the pro-slavery southern states. This tension eventually erupted into the Civil War.

St. Louis was also the starting point for a famous expedition. In 1804, Meriwether Lewis and William Clark set out from the city to explore the territory of the Louisiana Purchase. St. Louis is now known for its architecture, including the magnificent Gateway Arch.

Graceland, in Memphis, Tennessee, is the former home of Elvis Presley. Graceland attracts millions of visitors each year and provides a huge amount of tourist business for the local economy.

Memphis

Memphis, Tennessee, takes its name from an ancient Egyptian city. It is the largest city in Tennessee and one of the world's leading markets for lumber and cotton. Memphis is also home to the National Civil Rights Museum, which traces the history of the civil rights movement and honors the life of one of the movement's most important leaders, Dr. Martin Luther King, Jr. Another "king" associated with Memphis is Elvis Presley, the "King of Rock 'n' Roll." Elvis lived in Tennessee from the age of thirteen and started his famous career in a Memphis recording studio. Music plays a central role in the cultural life of Memphis, and the city is considered the birthplace of both the blues and rock 'n' roll.

New Orleans

Like the jazz music for which it is famous, New Orleans is an incredible blend of different styles and cultures. The city belonged first to France and then to Spain, before finally becoming part of the United States. During the city's French, Spanish, and American periods, different groups came to settle in Louisiana.

The French and Spanish settlers brought African slaves with them, and jazz is a living reminder of the influence of African Americans in New Orleans. Later, after Louisiana became part of the United States, Irish, Italian, and German **immigrants** all settled in New Orleans. Today, the city continues to attract people from a wide range of different racial backgrounds.

New Orleans is known for its distinctive architecture, particularly in its famous French Quarter. Impressive examples of New Orleans architecture include Jackson Square and the Pontalba apartment buildings.

The city is probably most famous for an annual celebration called Mardi Gras, or "Fat Tuesday." Many Christians around the world give up something they enjoy during Lent, which is a period of forty days, beginning with Ash Wednesday, before Easter. Mardis Gras lasts up to two weeks before Ash Wednesday. It is a time of parties, parades, and carnivals. People from around the world come to New Orleans to join the fun.

> *New Orleans is always a fun place to go, but it really comes alive for Mardi Gras. The floats, the costumes, the parades — they're all sensational. I wouldn't miss it for the world.*
>
> New York City resident

These revelers are celebrating Mardi Gras, a huge party that takes place in New Orleans every year. New Orleans has a mix of different cultures, and they all take to the streets to celebrate Mardi Gras.

Chapter 4

ECONOMIC ACTIVITY

ECONOMIC ACTIVITY

Modern Shipping

During World War I and World War II, many improvements were made to the boats shipping goods on the Mississippi River. Larger storage areas, more powerful engines, and advances in **navigation** helped make shipping one of the most profitable industries on the river. Today, the Mississippi River is the busiest inland shipping route in the United States. Every year, more than 90 million tons (81 million metric tons) of cargo are shipped along the Mississippi River. Typical loads include grain, coal, iron, steel, and gravel.

Most of the goods transported on the river are carried by barges — wide, flat boats, without engines, that can hold large amounts of goods. On the Mississippi River, several barges are typically roped together, and a diesel-powered boat then pushes the barges up or down the river. North of St. Louis, tows can push no more than fifteen barges at one time. Below St. Louis, however, tows are allowed to push many more barges.

> **" *...who could have imagined that Mississippi traffic would make such a comeback?* "**
> Mississippi River lockmaster

An Efficient Industry

The key to the success of the Mississippi River shipping industry is efficiency. A tow pushing 50 barges, for instance, can carry

as much cargo as 700 railroad cars or about 3,000 trucks. Even the fifteen-barge limit above St. Louis still allows vast amounts of cargo to be transported. For a freight train to carry the same amount of grain as fifteen barges, it would have to be 3 miles (4.8 km) long! Since barge traffic can transport such massive amounts of cargo, it has been the ideal solution for some unusual shipping jobs. Since the 1960s, for example, barges have been the method of choice when shipping the enormous booster rockets used to launch spacecraft.

Shipping on the river also has advantages for the environment. Barge shipping uses less fuel and creates less pollution than other means of shipping. Transportation by ship also helps ease the strain on crowded highways. For these reasons, businesses that use barges have been encouraged to continue using the Mississippi.

A single boat can push the massive load of many barges. Transportation by barge is inexpensive and causes relatively little environmental damage.

Farming

The Mississippi River basin contains rich farmland, and areas around the Upper Mississippi are particularly fertile. Minnesota has vast fields of wheat, while Wisconsin is famous for its dairy farming, leading the nation in the production of milk, eggs, and butter. Iowa is well known for its corn. The state is in the center of the "corn belt," a region of the Midwest where corn was once the most important crop. By the 1950s, however, farmers in the corn belt began to grow other crops, such as soybeans, along with corn.

Before the Civil War, cotton was the most important crop in the Lower Mississippi basin. The city of Memphis, for example, was largely built with fortunes made from cotton picked by slaves. After the Civil War, when slave labor ended, the cotton industry went into decline, forcing farmers to cultivate rice, soybeans, and other alternative crops. Today, Memphis is still a center of cotton production, but machines do the harvesting.

> "*...the South needed some commercial crop adapted to the climate, demanded by the overseas market, and suitable for production in circumstances ranging from the frontier farm to the great plantation.*"
> Historian Albert Cowdrey discussing the cotton boom in the 1800s, *This Land, This South: An Environmental History* (1983)

In some states, land near the Mississippi River is used for animal farming rather than for growing crops. Here, cattle graze in a Wisconsin field.

Fishing

The Mississippi River has always been a reliable source for all kinds of fish, particularly catfish. Recent changes to the Mississippi have resulted in new fish arriving in the river. The rise of the sea level in the Gulf of Mexico has sent a number of saltwater species, including shrimp and crabs, into the mouth of the Mississippi. The availability of these species in the delta swamps has led to a boom in the fishing industry.

Commercial fishing in the Mississippi is carefully controlled. Catfish are protected by law — any catfish shorter than 15 inches (38 centimeters) has to be thrown back in the river. Regulations for fishing are vital for maintaining fish stocks. When fish are caught in large numbers, they often do not have a chance to reproduce.

The Mississippi River passes through rich farmland, such as this huge field of wheat in Minnesota.

Manufacturing

The Mississippi basin has a long history of building things. Just as the original Native inhabitants of the Mississippi basin used trees to create their canoes, European settlers used lumber from the pine forests of the Upper Mississippi basin to construct their homes.

Large-scale manufacturing requires a lot of space, and many manufacturing companies have established themselves in smaller cities and towns along the Mississippi River rather than in large cities such as St. Louis or New Orleans. Moline, Illinois, is home to the headquarters of Deere & Company, the largest farm equipment manufacturing company in the world. The company operates three manufacturing plants in Moline and neighboring East Moline and employs more than 10,000 people in the area.

Wickliffe, Kentucky, is the location of the Westvaco paper manufacturing plant. In Spring Hill, Tennessee, General Motors owns a plant employing roughly 7,000 employees. In 1996, the Canadian steel company Ipsco opened a mill in Muscatine, Iowa, that cost approximately $425 million to build and employs about 400 people.

Shipbuilding is one of the biggest manufacturing industries on the southern parts of the Mississippi River, especially in Louisiana. This boat, which is on its way to a shipyard, is riding piggyback on another boat.

COCA-COLA

Today, most people sip Coke from cans or bottles. Originally, however, Coke was only served from soda fountains, and it was not put into bottles until 1894. The first person to bottle Coke was Joseph A. Biedenharn, who lived in Vicksburg, Mississippi, on the banks of the Mississippi River. He owned the Biedenharn Candy Company, and the store where he sold bottled Coke still stands — it is now the Biedenharn Museum of Coca-Cola.

The success of manufacturing in the Mississippi basin creates a demand for ships, and Louisiana is a particularly successful shipbuilding state. Many kinds of vessels are built in the shipyards of Louisiana — coast guard cutters, barges, fishing boats, and river patrol boats. Avondale Shipyards, located on the Mississippi River near New Orleans, is Louisiana's largest industrial employer.

Louisiana is the second biggest producer of oil in the United States, and it is the largest producer of natural gas. The state also has a large chemical industry. A number of chemicals and plastics are produced in factories in Baton Rouge, Louisiana, while thousands of offshore rigs drilling for oil in the Gulf of Mexico.

Pollution Problems

The development of the chemical industry in Louisiana has come at a price. The area between New Orleans and Baton Rouge is known as the "chemical corridor," a name that refers to the pollution of both the river and the air in this region. Pollution in the region has become so heavy that it is a highly visible problem — the borders of the chemical corridor are clearly marked by a thick, black fog.

In addition to its shipbuilding industry, Louisiana is known for its oil production. This huge oil refinery is located at Baton Rouge, Louisiana.

Chapter 5

ANIMALS AND PLANTS

An Amazing Range

The Mississippi River basin has a variety of **ecosystems** that include more than 240 **species** of fish and more than 400 different species of wildlife.

Many animals found in and along the Mississippi River today are the same ones that provided the original settlers of the region with clothing and food. These animals include deer, elk, beaver, moose, black bears, foxes, raccoons, and wolves. Among the varieties of fish found in the Mississippi river are catfish, walleyes, carp, and sturgeon.

The various animal species of the Mississippi basin are dependent upon one another for food. Larger animals such as wolves hunt deer, while smaller animals such as raccoons catch fish from the river.

> *Here I passed six weeks pleasantly, investigating the habits of wild deer, bears, cougars, raccoons and turkeys, and many other animals.*
> Wildlife artist John James Audubon describing the area near Commerce, Missouri, in 1806

The swamps, bayous, and wetlands of the southern part of the Mississippi River are home to a variety of animals, such as the alligator. This young alligator is in the Jean Lafitte National Historic Park and Preserve, south of New Orleans.

Wildlife under Threat

Since European settlement began in the Mississippi River basin, human involvement with the region's wildlife has caused a lot of damage. Fur trappers were among the first people to inhabit the lands surrounding the Mississippi. These trappers killed thousands of the animals that are now protected in national and state parks.

The Mississippi alligator, which lives in the river's delta, has been badly affected by hunting. In the 1970s, products made from alligator skin were extremely popular, and so many alligators were hunted that they almost died out. Today, the Mississippi alligator is protected by law, and its numbers are once again on the rise.

Hunting is only a part of the wildlife problem. **Deforestation** has also caused much damage, with the collection of mosses, orchids, and other plants helping to destroy patches of forest where animals once lived. Victims of deforestation include the white-tailed deer and the wild turkey. Fish, meanwhile, have suffered from **overfishing** and from changes to the course of the Mississippi.

To prevent further destruction of wildlife and to reverse some of the harm caused in the past, five National Wildlife Refuges have been established along the Mississippi — the Upper Mississippi River National Wildlife and Fish Refuge and the Mark Twain, Trempealeau, Minnesota Valley, and Illinois River National Wildlife Refuges. Together, these refuges contain over 300,000 acres (122,000 hectares) of wooded islands, water, and wetlands along the Mississippi River.

Herds of moose live near the northern stretches of the Mississippi. Other animals that live in this region include muskrats, raccoons, beavers, otters, and white-tailed deer.

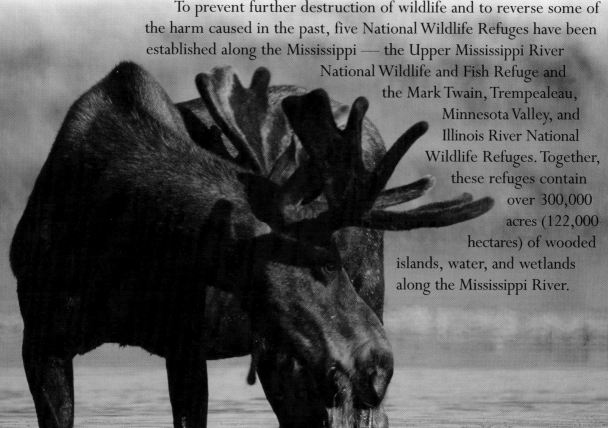

The Mississippi Flyway

Many birds fly south in late fall to spend the winter in a warmer climate. The birds then return to the north in the summer months to breed. This movement from north to south and back again is called **migration**. When birds migrate, they typically fly in groups over either the Atlantic or Pacific coasts or along one of two routes covering the midwestern United States. These migration routes are known as **flyways**.

The Mississippi flyway is the route traveled by 40 percent of North American waterfowl and shorebirds. An estimated 8 million ducks, geese, and swans spend the winter in the southern part of the flyway, and many more birds use it while traveling to South America. Scientists are not sure how the birds know the exact route they have to fly, but they do it every year.

From Canada, the Mississippi flyway crosses the Great Lakes and continues down the Mississippi River valley to the Mississippi delta. This route is popular among migrating birds for several reasons. First, the birds encounter few mountains, so they can fly freely without any detours. Second, the forests along this route provide cover from hunters — both animals and humans. Third, the vegetation along the flyway, such as sedges, pondweed, and millet, is an ideal source of food for the birds.

The bald eagle is one of the most distinctive birds in the United States. Bald eagles often breed along the banks of the Mississippi.

Birds that use the Mississippi flyway include snow geese, pelicans, herons, great white egrets, sparrows, ducks, cormorants, and blackbirds. Other creatures also use the flyway. The Monarch butterfly, for example, follows a similar migration pattern and spends its winters in the Gulf of Mexico.

> *"Humans must also do their part. We need to learn to watch, but not disturb...we want them [the birds] returning to their nesting sites in Wisconsin, Minnesota, and Canada, in good health. Therefore, we need to take a holistic [total] view...protecting the quality of the water and the fish, the air, the trees."*
> Wildlife specialist Pat Schlarbaum, quoted by Pat Middleton, *Eagle Watchers Celebrate the Come-Back Birds* (1999)

Problems on the Flyway

Although birds and butterflies spend much of their time in the air, they are just as affected by changes to the river basin's ecosystems as fish and other wildlife. Deforestation is particularly harmful, because birds and butterflies make their nests in trees on the rivers. A lack of trees results in fewer places to make nests.

These cormorants are resting in a tree before continuing their journey.

33

Chapter 6

ENVIRONMENTAL ISSUES

ENVIRONMENTAL ISSUES

> *I asked the dikeman what it would take to hold back the oncoming water. He told me glumly that it would take a miracle. When we woke up the next day, the levee had held.... The same day, water levels started to recede.*

Dave Doiron, resident of Prairie du Rocher, Illinois, describing the 1993 flood

Flooding Problems

For anyone who works on the Mississippi or lives near the river, floods are an ongoing concern. Even in the early days of European settlement on the Mississippi, floods were a problem. After New Orleans was founded in 1718, its settlers built a small levee to hold back the river water and protect their city.

In 1993, the Mississippi flooded large areas of land. This man was among thousands who suddenly found their homes under water. Many of the people affected lost almost everything they had in the disaster.

This structure is a flood control device on the Mississippi in Louisiana. These structures have been built in many locations along the Mississippi to stop its waters from spilling out onto surrounding lands after heavy rainfall.

Levees, Dams, and Reservoirs

After the devastating flood of 1927, the U.S. government committed itself to a complex flood control system for the Mississippi. This system involved the addition of many levees, which were made of concrete. Levees can be an effective defense against floodwaters. Occasionally, however, levees break, suddenly releasing thousands of gallons of water that can cause tremendous damage to nearby buildings and farmland.

    Adding levees and strengthening the ones already in place is the extent of what can be done to the Mississippi itself. The importance of the shipping industry on the river has prevented the massive construction needed to prevent flooding, because this construction would hinder transportation. Instead of focusing on the Mississippi, engineers have built dams and **reservoirs** on tributaries, such as the Kansas River. Reservoirs are useful because floodwaters can be stored in them and released at a later time.

    The main cause of any flood is too much rainfall. While the levees and channels worked well enough to handle flood conditions in 1945 and 1950, they failed in 1993. During the summer of 1993, extremely heavy rainfall caused the Mississippi to reach its highest recorded level — 48.49 feet (14.78 m) at St. Louis. This flood was possibly the most disastrous in the river's history.

THE FLOODS OF 1927 AND 1993

1927
246 people dead
700,000 made homeless
27,000 square miles (70,000 sq km) flooded
Approximately $4.4 billion in damage

1993
47 people dead
74,000 made homeless
15,600 square miles (40,400 sq km) flooded
Approximately $8 billion in damage

The United States Army Corps of Engineers

The United States Army Corps of Engineers (USACE), also known as the "Corps," is a team of roughly 35,000 expert scientists and engineers. One of the Corps' key responsibilities is the maintenance of the Mississippi River. Over the years, the Corps has worked to deepen the Mississippi River's channel, improve its water quality, and prevent it from flooding.

This model of the Mississippi has been built by scientists to test the effect of different amounts of water flowing down sections of the river.

THE USACE MISSISSIPPI RIVER MODEL

In Vicksburg, Mississippi, the United States Army Corps of Engineers has constructed a scale model of the Mississippi River. Using this model, scientists test new flood prevention plans before applying them to the river. The model can mimic the behavior of the river's waters in every possible situation.

> **" The scientific evidence is clear. Reconnecting the river to its floodplain and restoring seasonally flooded wetlands are essential to the health of the Mississippi River and reducing pollution. "**
> Rebecca Wodder, President of American Rivers, *Knight-Ridder, Tribune Business News*, May 9, 2001

This scientist is taking samples of the water in the Mississippi River. He will then test it for different types of pollution.

Conservation Questions

Occasionally, the methods of the Corps have drawn criticism from the general public. According to **conservation** groups, the Corps does not always operate with the best interests of the Mississippi River or its wildlife in mind. Conservationists argue that, because the Corps is a government agency, it is more concerned about improving the river for barge traffic than about doing what is best for the environment.

Some evidence exists to support these claims. The Corps is planning a major project to expand and rebuild the system of locks and dams on the river, for example, and this project will result in the further disturbance of fish and other wildlife in the Mississippi basin. It will also cost taxpayers more than a billion dollars. Conservation groups trying to block the rebuilding of the locks and dams include the Sierra Club, the Mississippi River Basin Alliance, and the Izaak Walton League.

Conservationists are also concerned about the effect that levees have on wildlife in the Mississippi basin. A growing number of environmentalists argue that, although flooding causes terrible damage, it plays an important part in maintaining the balance of the river's ecosystems. Floods help restore **wetlands** and even cut down on pollution. Wetlands act like sponges, absorbing pollutants in the air and the water before they have a chance to enter the river. Without floodwaters, however, the wetlands dry up.

Increasingly, conservation groups such as American Rivers, the Upper Mississippi River Conservation Committee, and the National Wildlife Federation are becoming involved in the future of the Mississippi River. While the members of these organizations clearly care about the Mississippi and the people who live on or near it, they do not always agree with the Corps about the methods that should be used to maintain the river.

Water Quality

More than 16 million people rely on the Mississippi River for their water, and the quality of the river's water supply is a major concern. There are two main threats to the river's water quality — nutrients, or food substances, and sediment. Nutrients include elements such as nitrogen and phosphorus, which find their way into the Mississippi through industrial and municipal waste and through farming. Fertilizers used in farming, for example, are full of nitrogen. Nitrogen triggers the growth of **algae** and pollutes the river water, making it unsuitable for drinking.

Sediment has always been in the Mississippi River, but what has changed in modern times is the amount. Before industrialization, the Mississippi River flowed strongly enough to move sediment south into the Gulf of Mexico. Modern industries, however, have created a level of sediment that the river cannot move. This sediment blocks sunlight from entering the river, killing fish and plants. The United States Army Corps of Engineers spends over $100 million every year to **dredge** the Mississippi and remove excess sediment.

Some portions of the Mississippi River are so badly contaminated that they fail to meet the goals of the Federal Clean Water Act passed by Congress in 1972. One particular area of concern is the Gulf of Mexico dead zone, a 7,000-square-mile (18,129-sq-km) area that stretches from the Mississippi River delta west to the Texas border. The waters in this area are highly polluted by nutrients that enter the Mississippi from midwestern farmlands and float south to the Gulf of Mexico. These nutrients have caused the amount of dissolved oxygen in the "dead zone" to be too low for water creatures and plants to survive.

THE ENVIRONMENTAL PROTECTION AGENCY

The Environmental Protection Agency (EPA) first began operating on December 2, 1970. The EPA's goal is to protect the natural environment, including air, water, and land. It consists of about 18,000 people in locations across the United States.

Taking Action

To address the environmental problems associated with the Mississippi River, the Environmental Protection Agency (EPA) has become involved. The EPA has been working with the states bordering the Mississippi to create a plan of action for cleaning up the river. The people who live in the cities and towns on the Mississippi are also making changes for the better. They are learning to save water and reduce their use of **pesticides** and other poisonous chemicals that can eventually flow into the river.

Today, the industries of the Mississippi River basin continue to pollute the river, as waste products from factories find their way into the water. The area shown in this photograph is known locally as "Cancer Alley," because people believe chemical pollution has caused an increase in cancer cases in the area.

Chapter 7

LEISURE AND RECREATION

Fun by the River

Like many famous landmarks, the Mississippi attracts many visitors. People from all over the world come to experience the sights and sounds of the river. Tourists support local economies by staying in hotels, eating in restaurants, and buying souvenirs.

Crowds watch a jazz trombonist march along Bourbon Street in New Orleans. Millions of tourists visit the city each year. Most of them end up on Bourbon Street, one of the city's biggest tourist attractions.

The Mississippi is an especially good destination for people who enjoy outdoor activities. Fishing on the Mississippi takes place all year long, and there are a number of spots along the river where people are allowed to hunt. Many visitors to the Mississippi enjoy camping and hiking, while biking and jogging are popular with people who live by the river.

Those who prefer being closer to the water can enjoy boating, kayaking, and water skiing. Some people even plan theme trips, using canoes to travel along the same passages first explored by pioneers such as Louis Jolliet and Jacques Marquette or Henry Rowe Schoolcraft.

Bird watchers love the Mississippi River because it is a flyway for so many North American birds. The legendary bald eagle often breeds along the banks of the Mississippi. Bald eagles are typically hard to find, but bird watchers who travel to the Mississippi can usually see them.

Festivals

In the summer months, numerous festivals are held on the shores of the Mississippi. Many of these festivals focus on the rich variety of music associated with the river. St. Louis is famous for its blues festival, which is held every September. New Orleans hosts its Jazz Fest, a ten-day celebration that attracts over 500,000 visitors each spring. There are also a number of Zydeco music festivals. Zydeco, a form of music dating back to the 1930s, was created by Creoles, French-speaking people of color descended from early French, Spanish, and African inhabitants of Louisiana. These festivals always include food. Spicy Creole dishes are a great favorite with visitors.

> 66 *New Orleans, that was a place where the music was as natural as the air. The people were ready for it like it was sun and rain.* 99
> Jazz musician Sidney Bechet, from *Treat It Gentle: An Autobiography* (1978)

The main attraction for any visitor to the Mississippi, however, is the river itself. For many people, just being able to see the incredible beauty of the Mississippi River firsthand is all the entertainment they need.

Museums of All Kinds

The Mississippi River has played an important role in the development of the United States. A reminder of the river's role can be found in many fine museums along its banks.

Dubuque, Iowa, is home to the Mississippi River Museum. This museum covers more than 300 years of the river's history. Key exhibits at the museum include live fish and turtles, Native American relics, a real captain's wheel, and Mud Island, an outdoor scale model of a stretch of the Mississippi River from Cairo, Illinois, to the Gulf of Mexico.

Possibly the most impressive exhibit at the Mississippi River Museum is the dredge *William M. Black*. The ship measures 277 feet (84 m) long and is one of the few steam-powered dredges to have survived unaltered to the present day. It was used between 1934 and 1973 to widen the channel connecting the Missouri River to the Mississippi River. Widening this channel was an especially important development for shipping during World War II.

Many visitors to the southern Mississippi region come to see the area's beautiful architecture. This house is on St. Charles Street in a wealthy district of New Orleans.

Ships on the River

More than a century has passed since steamboats were the common means of transportation along the Mississippi, but river cruises are still popular today. Some people travel along the river in houseboats. Many people, however, prefer to travel on replicas of old steamboats such as the *Delta Queen*, the *Mississippi Queen*, or the *Natchez*. The popularity of these steamboat replicas may in part be the result of Mark Twain's influence. Twain's books, especially *Life on the Mississippi*, make traveling slowly down the Mississippi River seem majestic and glamorous.

A more modern ship, the U.S.S. *Kidd*, is located in Baton Rouge, Louisiana. The U.S.S. *Kidd* is a destroyer — a small, fast combat ship outfitted with many weapons — that served in World War II. During the war, the *Kidd*, also known as the "Pirate of the Pacific," fought and won eight battles in the Pacific Ocean.

Reminders of History

Civil War enthusiasts enjoy visiting historic sites such as Vicksburg, in western Mississippi, which was the site of an important Civil War battle. The siege of Vicksburg led to the surrender of the Confederate forces in July 1863 and gave Union troops control of the Mississippi River.

Cotton plantations, located on the stretch of the Mississippi from south of Baton Rouge to New Orleans, provides another link to the past. The families who became wealthy from cotton often built giant mansions. Today, many people today flock to see these mansions, many of which have been turned into museums.

THE TRAIL OF TEARS

Cape Girardeau County, Missouri, is famous for the Trail of Tears State Park. In the 1830s, most Cherokee Indians lived in Georgia. When gold was discovered there, the Cherokees were forced to move, on foot, to Oklahoma. This long march, known as "The Trail of Tears," took place between October 1838 and March 1839. During the journey, thousands of Cherokee and other Native men, women, and children died. The Trail of Tears State Park honors the memory of Cherokees who crossed the Mississippi at this spot and those Cherokees who lost their lives during the march.

Chapter 8

THE FUTURE

THE FUTURE

This map shows the area that will be affected by the Yazoo Backwater Area Project, which is meant to drain Yazoo backwater wetlands in the event of a flood. Some people believe draining the wetlands will make them uninhabitable for wildlife.

New Plans

The Mississippi River will continue to play an important part in American life for many years to come. Proof of the Mississippi's importance can be found in plans that have been made for the river.

The United States Army Corps of Engineers, for example, recently announced plans for its Yazoo Backwater Area Project, which has been designed to drain floodwater from a 1,550-square-mile (4,015-sq-km) segment of the Lower Mississippi basin. If flooding occurs, water will be pumped out of flooded lands and then returned to the Mississippi once the river returns to normal levels. The Yazoo Project has been the subject of much discussion. Organizations such as the U.S. Fish and Wildlife Service are afraid the Yazoo Project will damage wetlands by removing too much water and making them uninhabitable for fish and wildlife. The Army Corps, however, insists the project's pumps will only be used during a flood.

Meanwhile, the departments of transportation in the states of Illinois and Missouri are planning a new river bridge. This bridge will be 222 feet (68 m) wide, with a total length of 3,150 feet (960 m) and towers up to 435 feet (133 m) high. It will cross the Mississippi just north of St. Louis, Missouri. The purpose of the new bridge is to ease traffic on the nearby Poplar Street Bridge, which is growing more crowded every day. The new bridge will have eight traffic lanes and additional room for another four. Construction is scheduled to begin in 2004.

> **" *The face of the water, in time, became a wonderful book — a book that was a dead language to the uneducated passenger, but which told its mind to me without reserve, delivering its most cherished secrets as clearly as if it uttered them with a voice. And it was not a book to be read once and thrown aside, for it had a new story to tell every day.* "**
> Mark Twain, *Life on the Mississippi* (1883)

The River Keeps Rolling

The Mississippi River is one of the United States' most precious natural resources, and it is also a link to the history of the nation. Pollution and neglect, however, could ruin the Mississippi for future generations. Fortunately, people are learning from past mistakes. As long as the Mississippi River is properly cared for, it will continue to be a vital lifeline running through the heart of the country.

As this photograph of the Mississippi at St. Louis shows, the river is still busy with traffic. The Mississippi River continues to play a vital role in the daily life of the United States.

GLOSSARY

algae: microscopic organisms that grow in water and can reduce oxygen levels in rivers.

basin: the area of land drained by a river and its tributaries.

conservation: the practice of managing and protecting a natural environment and its wildlife.

deforestation: the clearing of a forest.

delta: a flat, triangular area of land where a river empties into a large body of water, such as an ocean, through many channels.

dredge: to clear mud, sand, or rock from a river or bay so boats can travel more easily.

ecosystem: the environment of an area and all the living things in that environment.

flyway: a certain route taken by migratory birds every year.

glacier: a huge mass of slowly moving ice.

immigrant: a person who leaves one country to live permanently in another country.

levee: a raised area of land designed to hold back floodwater.

lock: a closed area on a river or canal, with gates at each end, that allows boats and ships to be raised or lowered to different water levels.

meanders: takes a winding course.

migration: a set pattern of travel, at certain times of the year, from one place to another.

mouth: the place where a river empties into a large body of water, such as an ocean.

navigation: the process of guiding a boat or ship on a body of water.

overfishing: catching so much of a fish species that it is in danger of dying out.

pesticides: chemicals used to kill insects that damage crops but are often harmful to wildlife and humans.

reservoir: a natural or artificial pond or lake that is used for storing water.

sediment: small pieces of soil and rock that are carried and deposited by a river.

service industry: businesses such as hotels, restaurants, and banks that provide services to people.

source: the point of origin for the waters of a river or stream.

species: a certain kind of animal or plant.

trading post: a site in a lightly settled region where people exchange local goods.

tributary: a small stream or river that feeds into a larger river.

wetlands: areas of land with extremely moist soil, often as a result of flooding.

FURTHER INFORMATION
FURTHER INFORMATION

TIME LINE

c. 12,000 years ago	The Mississippi River is formed during the last ice age.

A.D.

1000	Mississippian culture flourishes.
1400s	Mississippian culture disappears.
1539	Hernando de Soto finds the Mississippi River.
1673	Louis Jolliet and Jacques Marquette explore the Mississippi River.
1682	René-Robert Cavalier, Sieur de La Salle, claims the Mississippi River basin for France.
1783	Treaty of Paris declares the Mississippi River to be the western boundary of the United States.
1803	The Louisiana Purchase gives the United States possession of the Mississippi River basin.
1811	The first steamboat sails on the Mississippi River.
1832	Henry Rowe Schoolcraft finds the source of the Mississippi River.
1879	The Mississippi River Commission is created.
1927	First great Mississippi flood of the twentieth century.
1938	Proposal for the Great River Road Parkway.
1993	Second great Mississippi flood of the twentieth century.

BOOKS

Currie, Stephen. *The Mississippi*. (Lucent Books, 2002)

Hiscock, Bruce. *The Big Rivers: The Missouri, The Mississippi, and the Ohio*. (Atheneum, 1997)

Lourie, Peter. *Mississippi River: A Journey Down the Fathers of Waters*. (Boyds Mills Press, 2000)

Middleton, Pat. *Discover! America's Great River Road*. (Great River Publishing, 2000)

Mudd-Ruth, Maria. *The Mississippi River*. (Benchmark Books, 2000)

Pollard, Michael. *The Mississippi*. (Benchmark Books, 1997)

WEB SITES

American Rivers
www.amrivers.org/mississippiriver/default.htm
A history of the river, with information on water quality and river wildlife.

Great River Road
www.mississippiriverinfo.com
Travel and development information about states bordering the Mississippi.

Mississippi River Division
www.mvd.usace.army.mil
Site for the Mississippi Valley Division of the United States Army Corps of Engineers.

Mississippi River Home Page
www.greatriver.com
A list of books on the river and an overview of attractions in towns and along its banks.

U.S. Environmental Protection Agency
www.epa.gov
Information about the Mississippi from the U.S. government.

47

INDEX
INDEX

Numbers in **boldface** type refer to illustrations and maps.

alligators **30**, 31
Amish people 19, **19**
animals **27**, 30–33, **30**, **31**, **32**, **33**, 37, 38
Arkansas River 5, **6**, 10, 11, 13, **18**, **44**

barges 16, **16**, 24, 25, **25**, 29, 37
Baton Rouge, Louisiana 5, **18**, 29, **29**, 43
bayous 9, **9**, **30**
birds 32–33, **32**, **33**, 41

Cahokia, Illinois 12
Civil War 15, 19, 21, 26, 43
Clark, William 21
cotton 9, 22, 26, 43

dams 17, **17**, 35, 37
deforestation 31, 33
Driftless Region 6, 7

eagles **32**, 41
Environmental Protection Agency (EPA) 38, 39
explorers 8, 13, 21

farming 18, 18, 26, **26**, **27**, 38, 39
fish 27, 30, 31, 37, 42, 44
fishing 12, **12**, 27, 41
flooding and flood control 12, 17, **17**, 34–37, **34**, **35**, 44, **44**

Great Depression 16, 17
Great River Road Parkway 17
Gulf of Mexico 5, **6**, 7, 8, 9, 13, 14, **18**, 27, 29, 33, 38, 39

ice age 6, 7
industry 16, 28–29, 35, 38, **38**

jazz 23, **40**, 41
Jolliet, Louis 13, 41

King, Martin Luther, Jr. 22

Lake Itasca **6**, 8, **8**, 9, 11
Lake Superior 6, **6**, **7**, **18**
La Salle, René-Robert Cavalier, Sieur de 13, 14
Lewis, Meriwether 21
Louisiana Purchase 14, 21
lumber 20, 22, 28

Mardi Gras 23, **23**
Marquette, Jacques 13, 41
Memphis, Tennessee 5, 13, **18**, 22, **22**, 26
Minneapolis, Minnesota 5, **18**, 20, **20**
Mississippi delta **6**, 7, 9, **9**, 10, 27, 31, 32, 38
Mississippi River Commission 17
Missouri River 4, 5, **6**, 10, **10**, **18**, 42
museums 17, 22, 42, 43

Native Americans 4, 12, **12**, 13, 20, 28, 42, 43
New Orleans, Louisiana 5, 14, 18, **18**, 23, **23**, 29, **30**, 34, **40**, 41, **42**, 43

oil 29, **29**

plants 31, 38
pollution 25, 29, 33, 36, 37, **37**, 38, **38**, 39
Presley, Elvis 22

railroads 15, **15**, 25

Schoolcraft, Henry Rowe 8, 41
sediment 5, 6, 7, 10, 38
ships and boats **10**, 14, **14**, 15, 16, **16**, 19, 20, 24–25, **25**, **28**, 29, 35, 42, 43
slaves 21, 23, 26
Soto, Hernando de 13, **13**
St. Anthony Falls **6**, 9, 20
St. Louis, Missouri 5, 10, 18, **18**, 20, 21, **21**, 24, 41, 35, 45, **45**
St. Paul, Minnesota 5, 11, **18**, 20
steamboats 14, **14**, 15, 16, 19, 20, 43

tourism 18, **22**, 40, **40**
transportation 14, 15, 16, 18, 24–25, 35, 43
Twain, Mark 15, 19, 43, 45

U.S. Army Corps of Engineers (USACE) 36, 37, 38, 44

wetlands 36, 37, 44
World War I 16, 24
World War II 16, 24, 42, 43

Yazoo Backwater Area Project 44, **44**

DATE			